SETTING SALES

10 EASY STEPS TO A

SUCCESSFUL

CAREER IN SALES

WRITTEN BY
ROBERT RUSSO

SETTING SALES

SETTING SALES

SET THE COURSE AND RIDE THE WAVE TO ACHIEVING SUCCESS IN SALES

After many years of success in sales, my wife, friends and colleagues encouraged me to write a book. They said write a book that explains what it is I do so people who lack experience, training or just lack the basic skills can emulate what I do. It should also be useful to someone with experience to help them to obtain better results. It should be helpful as an outline to look back for a tune up or to recharge the sales approach. Keep it short and to the point they said. I'm not a writer I'm a Salesman but in this case they sold me. So here it is my short how to. I hope you find it helpful.

This is not a book on how to get rich from a career in sales, although it could be, that's up to you. I will tell you, I am happy with what I have been able to attain through my ability to close sales. I am never concerned on how to make money, no matter how poor the economic climate. I am confident that I will always be able to make and get what I want or need. In my lifetime, I have been through some financial challenges. No matter how deep the challenge, I have always been able to sell my way out of the difficulty. By applying the basic selling principles outlined in this book I am confident that anyone can achieve confidence and a true feeling of being independent and secure for life.

DEDICATION

I dedicate this book to all those who prodded me and sold me on the idea that I could do this. I especially want to thank my wife and best friend, Peggy, who always stands solidly behind me, in good times and bad, including all those hard years of trial by error. She gave me the belief and confidence in all that I have ever done. She is the ultimate friend, wife and mother. I also wish to acknowledge my three children. I am very proud of you all and the fact that you are all very accomplished and productive young adults.

CONTENTS

MY INTRODUCTION TO SALES

The year 1954, the place Bronx, New York, and a five year old sees an opportunity. That's my first recollection of my beginnings in sales. We lived in a two story brick home on the second floor, it was Mom, Dad, my Brother and I. The event that led to my first encounter was the announcement my Mom and Dad had made to my brother and me. Great news, we were getting a little sister. My Mom and Dad had adopted my precious Sister. They told us that they were bringing her home on that Saturday. Armed with this news what would you expect a five-year-old salesmen to do. So the day arrived, we were all so excited, it was very early when we went to pick her up and bring her home.

What happens next I can remember like it was yesterday. After being disturbed by some noise outside, just about noon my Dad stepped out of the house onto the second floor porch. With a roar I could hear, "ROBERT WHAT IS GOING ON!" as he witnessed a line of kids leading down the two flights of stairs to the sidewalk below.

Yep you guessed it, in the days leading up to the arrival I had sold, for a nickel a piece, admission to come see the new baby sister. A star was born. Unfortunately my dad made me give the money back and send the kids on their way!

ACKNOWLEDGEMENTS

My special thanks to wife Peggy, my sister Linda, daughter Kim and to Charlotte without your many hours of help in editing and formatting this book it would still be in the hot tub room on the chair, in the a pile of notes on paper.

I also want to thank the many mentors and sales professionals that I have worked with and trained over my many years in sales. Lastly to all of the clients that I have had the pleasure to be involved with, I have to say thank you for listening to me and for purchasing what I had to sell.

SETTING SALES

1 - SETTING SALES

It has been said that a great sales person is born naturally. I believe that is true. The difference is I believe every one of us was born with the ability to be successful in sales.

For as long as I can remember, I understood that if I ever wanted to get something someone else had, I had to ask for it. I also remember that there were many times I asked for something and I was told no. What I did then and need to do now in order to make the sale is to turn that no into a yes. Think of all the creative ways you may have handled overcoming the no, the objection or rejection when getting a no. I promise I will do my homework; I will keep my room clean, and walk the dog and so on. Basically you instinctively or naturally negotiated and manipulated, you offered items or services for the exchange, and you presented your case. You did this naturally by tapping into an emotion of the person in front of you, your prospect. It worked most of the time and in essence you were making (closing) a sale.

We did not always get what we wanted, at least not right away. I am sure some of us did give in quicker then others. Those of us, who pressed on, would have closed the deal more then the others. That persistence is in my opinion the essence of who is best at selling.

The truth is that the fundamentals of making sales are simple. Know what you want, ask for it, handle or overcome the objection, ask for it again. We all survived the ultimate denial as kids we all failed to get what we wanted, all of the time. The fact is that when we are involved in selling we can never, no matter how good we are get every sale to conclude in a yes. The really good salesperson knows this, and not only handles a no, they understand that no is part of the process. A no is most often the way to a yes. After all, a no is at least a conclusion of a sale, a no is a whole lot better than a maybe. I for one am glad when I get a no, because I truly believe that every no I get brings me closer to my next yes. If you accept this as fact, we are in the same boat, so take the ride as we "Set Sales".

As we Set Sale, I will on the pages that fallow lay out a chart, in simple terms, an outline or a step-by-step formula that I have learned and always use in getting the sale. I will site examples of how each step in the process should go, the purpose and why they are necessary. As in everything in life there is nomenclature to describe certain forms or techniques. I will give some examples, as needed but that is not the purpose of this book. I will be limiting myself on defining a technique. I will concentrate on emphasizing the words and methods needed to master that technique.

The majority of my sales have been related to selling goods and services in the home industry. Most of the examples will be from experiences I have had, so naturally they will for the most part lean toward that industry. Those examples are easily convertible to your particular product or service.

Much of the knowledge contained in this book has come from my hands on experiences and by association with a wide range of professionals and peers. I have also attended numerous professional sales trainings and a countless number of sales meetings and seminars, each have created the sum of the total. I have sold door-to-door, business-to-business, in retail shops, in function halls and at fair grounds. I have sold wholesale and retail and have experience in, one on one and in large group atmospheres. In all of the above, the basics are and remain the same.

The business of sales are classified and defined in many different ways. However defined, the basic principals will apply no matter the classification. Knowing the different classifications will help you find your area of comfort and may enhance your ability to succeed. Let's look at a few of those classifications. In Retail sales, generally a consumer will seek you out in response to an advertisement in an effort to satisfy a need or a want. It is important that you know this, so you can uncover that need or want and then satisfy it. Almost a complete opposite to retail will be the wholesale sale. This type of sale is made on the basis of your finding the proper person or outlet for your product or service, you are creating and selling the need. Then there are real estate sales, insurance, financial or investments, technical, and more. The classification really has no bearing on the basics, as I said it would help to know them and then choose for yourself which will work for you. In your effort to learn from this book, the sales process or the order of the parts may be somewhat modified but the total sum of the parts should stay the same. I also want to point out that the venue for sales will vary. The steps shouldn't change, even when they are used in sales by engaging the prospects in a business-to-business, door-to-door, in a store or in their home. Then consider there is the street vender, phone solicitor or the telemarketer, the same steps will apply. Some sales are warm calls, this is when through some sort of previous connection the prospect knows you are coming. Another side is the cold call. This is just the opposite of the warm call in that the prospect has no idea who you are, prior to your meeting. Still the steps remain the same.

In all of these sales classifications or venues you will encounter a constant element that is the one ingredient that will make or break your success. As long as you follow the steps laid out in this guide you will be successful and forever be increasing in your sales ability.

There is one major caution that you must avoid. That is Fear. Do not allow this sales killer to board your sales boat. Fear is the one emotions you need to get rid of, dump it overboard. You should control and make use of all the other emotion, such as Joy, turn joy into enthusiasm. You should turn anger into intensity or tenacity, disappointment and rejection are a part of the business, turn them into desire, a challenge for perseverance. Fear however is a stopper.

If there is one thing I have leaned during my years of sales it is that there is no room or reason for fear. If you follow the steps, and you are prepared you should be fearless in your approach to getting the sale. I will share with you this fear creating experience. I early on in my life when first starting out in sales used to fall into a bad habit that developed into fear for me. I was young and just beginning my journey in my sales career I was a bit more serious and involved with my friends and social calendars then I like to admit. Every now and then shall we say I dropped the anchor way too soon! If I was to make a follow up call at a set time and was acting irresponsibly for the reasons mentioned above, I would procrastinate and put off the follow up, to the point that at times I never did follow up. Needless to say I did not get those sales, worse I will never know if I could have. I now know the reason I did not follow up. It was Fear that kept me from making those follow up calls. I was afraid of rejection and the reprimand caused by the delay due to my failure to execute on my commitments. Since those early days I have learned that you should make follow up a priority. Even when you mess up, it is okay to admit your error. Do not let the fear of your consequences dictate your success or failure. Since those early days, I have lost a sale or two because of poor follow up, but for the most part I learned that it is better to be late with a follow up and face the consequences rather then live in fear of those consequences and never call at all. The same rule applies if you accidentally gave some wrong information. Bite the bullet and admit to your mistake and move on. Another sure torpedo that will sink your sale every time is if you are not truthful with yourself or your prospect. If you make a statement or a promise that you cannot make good on, it will not only come back to haunt you with that prospect, it can hurt with future prospects as well. Remember that in all cases people talk to each other and they love to relate their experiences good and bad to each other. If you try to kid yourself in the process by offering mis-truths, you will allow for the number one killer, fear to take you off your course. The fear of being caught will enter into your sale and will most assuredly end any chance for long-term success.

My background includes training in overcoming objection; need satisfaction sales, open and closed probing, understanding feature and benefit sales. I am skilled in many closing techniques such as the Pie Technique, Ben Franklin and Cost vs. Value just to name a few. I studied and completed a course with Mark M. Barkan, A.S.T.D. This is a professional development program designed to work with different personalities. While representing an Arkansas based Furniture Manufacture, one of the nations leading furniture manufacturers, I was (based on my sales performance) asked to address the sales force, of over 100 representatives at a national sales meeting. The subject was "creative closing techniques for a changing market." At this meeting I introduced an advertising campaign that was sold successfully to dealers across the nation. The theme was "The Dawn of a New Selling Day." In fact each sales call is a new opportunity, or a new selling day, and I prepare myself the same way, each and every time.

As you navigate through this book I ask you to ask, "Does this make sense" if so use it. If not ask how you would do it differently and if you think that makes sense and it works great. If not just try it my way, what do you have to lose?

I would encourage you to attend as many sales seminars and self help improvement programs as you can. To this day whenever I attended and or run a sales meetings, I always look to find something I never heard or thought of, something that adds to my sales process in a positive way. One last statement that is key I will repeat this over and over through out, and want you to know before setting out to sell. Remember this, it is always about the client or prospect it is never about or for you.

2 - THE PRE-SALE

The Pre-sale, is the starting point, the Dock of the Bay if you will, with one exception Isolation, which I will expand on later, the pre-sale is as important in the steps to the sale, as are all the other steps. All the steps are important. Each will contribute to your successful conclusion. The pre-sale will have more components and generally take more time then the others. While most of the other steps may be less rigid in their order and can sometimes be altered in sequence, the pre-sale must in each presentation be the first step.

As the name would indicate the pre-sale is made up of all those things you must learn or do prior to the actual sales call. Simply put this is your Preparation. The Pre-sale will be physical, mental even spiritual.

Basic training; I cannot express enough how important it is to know everything you can about your market, product or service. Ask yourself some simple questions, what is it, what will it do, why would I need or want it, who else has it or something like it, how is it the same, how is it different, what does it cost, is there value, long-term will it appreciate or depreciate. As the possibilities are somewhat endless if you're new to selling it would be wise to seek advice from those who have set sale before you and learn from those people. Seek out only those people who are positive and optimistic about what they do. Learn all you can about your company and those who would compete with you.

While one team may be better on paper then another they do not always win, that is why the game is played. The team or player that usually wins, given they are in the same playing field are those who are better prepared. I have through my years heard other salespersons say that another salesperson was lucky. Luck has nothing at all to do with it, being prepared and capitalizing on the mistakes or faults of others will beat luck every time.

Another part of the pre-sale is the mental and spiritual preparation. The mental is reviewing all that you have learned thinking through the process. Recall not only from what you have learned from others also draw on past experiences. Whenever possible remember those things that may have presented a problem to you. Define and strategize your objectives. Several companies I have been associated with will offer spiritual uplifting affirmations. I believe affirmations are a huge part of the pre-sale. There are many pre-written affirmations and you can find books of affirmations or web sites that offer all types of affirmations. I will tell you that over the years I have created a few affirmations of my own, and you could do the same. The main thing is that before you greet or meet the prospect you need to get ready to do what ever it takes to get the job done.

Know your arena, the area you will compete in, and your market, research it and learn. Update yourself on the facts constantly. It is in all cases a good thing to be well versed on current events, trends and what is going on in your selling area. Know where you are going and arrive ahead of time. I am sure you heard of the great coach and motivator the late Vince Lombardi well you might not know that he operated on what is known as Lombardi Time. According to Coach Lombardi if you did not report to a scheduled event at least fifteen minutes early, you were considered to be late!

At this point you can begin to see there is nothing hard about the pre-sale, other then it takes time and effort and you need to pay attention to the details.

Assuming that I have been properly trained to sell a particular brand of vinyl siding, also assume I have knowledge about all of the key elements of the product, the competition and markets. That said this is an example of a pre-sale routine that I would perform prior to moving on to the next step what I define as the Entry.

My pre-sale generally starts the night before. I will at some point before going to bed look at my appointment book to make sure I know all the locations and times that I have scheduled for the next day. I will see that I have all the tools I will need to perform the business of selling. Are my product samples clean and neat ready to show? Do I have all the supporting literature or catalogs and do I have proper writing tools and materials?

This is important. You must have everything you need ready, and you should never have to concern yourself during your presentation in thinking that you are not prepared. It is fundamental to have them. I can tell you that I learned this the hard way. I had successfully navigated myself to a positive conclusion I worked for three hours on a new kitchen layout. I made a sale only to find that when I reached in my briefcase to pull out the agreement that I had used the last one the day before. I had to leave without the proper paperwork. When I called to confirm the time I was to go back to write the contract they had a change of heart. Obviously what happened is they lost confidence in me. Pretty costly basic mistake, one I never made again.

The day of a call, I will arrive in the area at least a half-hour ahead of schedule. I would first do a drive by to get a look at the house. Since I was selling siding I wanted to get an idea of the size of the house, and I would want to compare its condition to other houses in the area. I would also try to see tell tale signs about the people inside. I would look to see a new car, a boat; did they have a pool, a play set for kids. Did they need or already have other improvements done like a roof or windows. I would look at the rest of the neighborhood to see if any other houses compared with theirs, I would note a good example of a properly sided home versus maybe one that was not done so well. I would look for other homes that needed work and make a note of the addresses and names if I could. During the course of working with the prospect all of this preparation is important. The most important of course were the houses that needed work; I would want to know if they knew the homeowners so I could get a referral.

I would arrive back at the prospects home and I would begin the spiritual pre-sale routine. I never wanted to gain entry before I cleared my mind of any negative or disruptive thoughts. You can't bring your personal baggage or problems and or misfortunes to the sale process. Throw out any preconceived notions; make no assumption other than the assumption of the positive, you will make the sale. The next and very last thing to do is your affirmation, get pumped, commit to yourself that you are willing to do whatever it takes to gain your objective. A last note on the process of being positive, at the conclusion of the process, someone will be getting the sale either you sell them or they will sell you on not getting it done. Since you are the professional who has done all the pre-sale requirements it should be you who wins more often then not. Now that this is understood it means nothing without the next step, "The Entry".

3 - GAINING ENTRY

It should be obvious that the entry must take place before any other step after the pre-sale. If you cannot get access to your prospect you are done. There is more to the entry then you may think, and it will vary depending on the type of sale and the sales environment. I will elaborate more on the ways to gain entry, as it pertains to the different types of sales or sales environment, as we navigate our way in this step.

Simply stated, if selling in home, entry is being courteous and respectful of the homeowner's property. To gain entry you may need to check all doors; front, side, and rear. Don't assume by ringing a doorbell and when no one answers or opens a door that no one is there. More often then not they may not have heard the bell, they may be in the storage closet or on the phone or working in a noisy environment. Do whatever you must to get in, knock maybe the bell is not working. Today we all have cell phones a very good tool to gain entry, do not call the prospect, call someone else and have them make the call. As a part of entry I will tell you that I think it is important that you are thinking positive and that your prospect wants you to be there. If you think that way you will gain access and you also will be more confident once you do.

On more than one occasion I tried a front door, then a side door, only to walk to the back yard and found the prospect talking to the neighbor, usually telling them that I was coming to talk to them about new siding. I can tell you that several times I sold the neighbor as well.

The only real difference in the entry as it pertains to the different types of sale is between that of a warm sale versus the cold call. In the warm call you are expected and you will hopefully be able to complete the process from beginning to conclusion. In the cold call you have to be mindful that no one is expecting you. You should still try to gain access but you should keep in mind that the success of your visit may be in that you were able to extract information to be able to gain access or entry at a later date. You have to consider that your attempt at entry has set the stage for a future warm call and a full entry. Now when I say at a later time it could be that you found the name of the person or business, you look up the phone number, you call and you are in, you now prospected successfully. Do whatever it takes, there is not much to it, other than to be positive and just to do it.

4 - WARM UP

The warm up is designed to build trust and confidence as it breaks down the barriers between you and the prospect. It is vitally important that this step be accomplished. There are some companies and salespeople that believe that in today's hustle bustle that there is no time for warm up. I could not disagree more about that.

I will say this is one of the steps that does not have to be done at the point laid out in the outline. It is of course better if it can be done in the order set out but it is not necessary. Warming up can't be forced or appear to be contrived in any way. It can take some people a bit longer than others. The most important thing to be noted about the warm up is that you should never ever think about presenting price or closing until you have accomplished warm up.

The purpose of the warm up is to gain a comfort level with the prospect. In the process of making the sale you will need to be able to extract information of a personal and or private nature. People will exchange information like income or budget or credit worthiness from people they like or trust. Without warm up confidence and trust, an exchange attempting to obtain personal information just can't happen, without having to over come a huge resistance.

Warming up is not as difficult as you may think. The most important element in the warm up is to be natural. Use all the tools at your disposal but keep it real. Go back for a moment to the pre-sale. Remember if you did that step as described you are a diverse person with knowledge on current events and the environment you are in. Keep religion and politics off limits. With men and more and more now with women as well, sports and community activities are good icebreakers. When you looked in the driveway did you see a nice car or if they had a boat, people love to talk about their possessions and it is another way to get them talking. Take a look around the house or the office at maybe a trophy, an award, a fish tank or a work of art. The main thing is to be genuine, do not be artificial and by all means do not claim to be an expert in a topic you know little about.

Once you have found that common ground or subject that has enabled you to brake down the barriers, you now must be cautious not to over stay your time in the warm up mode. You must create a balance here between too much and too little. Too much warm up and you made a friend but not a sale, this is not good. You can tell if you did not warm up enough if you get some resistance to the inquiry of personal or private information. It is okay for you to go back and spend a little more time on warm up. It is better to do that then to never get out of warm up.

An example of how simple a warm up can happen. I was working as the sales manager of a very upscale furniture store in Westchester

County, New York. I happened to be walking past the stores main entrance on my way to my office, I was walking past a man and well dressed woman, The man was a very large man dressed in all black, he had a black tee shirt with shortened sleeves about three quarter, his arms were draped in silver bracelets and he was wearing a black cape. Instead of saying what I hear more then I can stand "Can I help you?" as I believe this is the worst opening statement and hardly ever establishes a working bond, I was honest, and sincere and with a smile I said "I am not so sure I get the look but I absolutely admire your courage". This precipitated a real belly laugh from the man and the woman. His first response was to ask me my name he then told me his. He then told me with out my asking why he was in our showroom and asked me if I could work with him. I won't reveal his name but I will tell you that as it turned out he was one of the stage directors of the Metropolitan Opera. He explained that he was working on decorating the Park Avenue apartment for a Metropolitan Opera star. She was still in Europe. It was a most lucrative and totally exciting experience with the topper being a write up in the New Yorker magazine.

The best part of how this warm up went is that the prospect took us out of warm up and into the next step when he volunteered what he came in for. He took us to the work phase. Remember that you are there to work with them so you need to make a transition from warm up back to work mode. You can do that best by asking Qualifying questions and by making a transitional statement.

In example "many of my regular clients came in this week to see me because they had seen our current promotion on TV, is that why you are here today?" Wait for the response and you are on your way to the next step, Qualify, or to engage in wants and needs.

5 - QUALIFY

Qualifying is the first step to doing business, it is the transition from warm up to the business mode. In this step you will discover many necessary facts and get answers to pertinent questions. If you are not in the appropriate place to conduct your business now is the time to direct your prospect to that place to do so. It is also the time to take out all of the paper work and documents that are needed to move forward and to conclude the sale. A very important item to have in front of you is a note pad. You should make notes through out the process, those notes will be used later in the closing, and in a subtle way it shows that you care.

Some of the questions you will be asking in qualifying are; How long has the prospect been looking into this, do they have knowledge of the product or service, you need to see if they are driven by price, quality, performance or by all three, find out when do they want it? See what competition there may be, if any.

Now would be a good time to get a sense of the prospects financial circumstance or condition. It would not make a whole lot of sense to go on with a presentation only to find out two hours later that they have no money or credit.

I cannot re-emphasize enough how important the warm up was, you can see now how it is needed in order to set up qualifying and in order to uncover the financial and personal information.

I have always been able to be frank and up front with my prospects in uncovering this information why, because I do such a good job in the warm up. I like to be truthful and I use real life experiences when probing for the information. I will use one real life experience that happened to me many years ago while I was still in high school. I had been working part time at a furniture outlet store. It was a nasty cold and rainy Saturday in New Rochelle, New York. Some time in the late morning a rather scruffy looking man in a somewhat soiled London Fog raincoat, stopped and stood in an enclosed overhang by the entrance to the store. I watched him for a while, he looked wet and cold. I was after a short time comfortable with approaching him and asked if he wanted to come into the store for a while to warm up. He thanked me and came in. A short time later he asked me about the nature and history of the store. I explained that we were a warehouse outlet store for one of the area's better furniture stores, and that we sold merchandise at greatly reduced prices. He began asking questions regarding delivery and pricing on several large items. Now mind you this guy did not look like he could afford the delivery charge let alone the furniture. As it turned out he was a very famous photographer and wound up furnishing a townhouse he had just purchased. I learned from this early on not to judge a person's wealth on looks alone. I don't relate this story to prospects every time but I do tell them that at an early age, I found out that you can not tell what a person can afford or what they are comfortable in paying just by looking at them, so I ask, Mr. or Mrs. Prospect, how do you normally pay for items like this? That question will invoke all kinds of useful information. An example of such a response that is said quite often is they will tell you they will be paying in cash. Although cash is nice I have found that when people make large purchases they usually want to pay in cash if their credit is not so good. I want to make this perfectly clear that just because a prospect has limited cash and their credit is poor, it is no reason to fold up and leave. It is more often to your advantage when credit is an issue. If you know the credit situations before you try to close, you can use a resource for creative financing to close the sale. The key is to gather all this information before you conclude with qualifying. Once you are satisfied that you extracted what you need from qualifying, it is time to do what I believe you must do more then anything else, this is the Pre-Close.

6 - PRE-CLOSE

The Pre-Close is designed to invoke several necessary components, the most important being the way to establish control. By control I mean control of the process not the prospect. For the most part I use this time to do what I am there to do, to turn warm up and qualifying into the sale's process.

Getting out the information you want to be conveyed and doing it in a story like manner will allow you the means to take control, again not of the prospect but of the process, The story should and will be flexible and personalized to each personality you will encounter. You can, if you are and you should be prepared to confidently show the prospect that you know what you are doing. You have knowledge, you are an expert and you use this to gain the confidence in you. This is the confidence that the prospect will need in making a decision. The story should first tell about your company, give the history, accomplishments and why it is a company that can do what the prospect needs it to do. I will then give my story, my background how I came to be with the company or how I came to do what it is I do. I will also use this step to see how well I did in warm up. Did I accomplish my goal to gain their respect, and trust. At the very least I should have the prospects trust. Remember you will need that trust to get the private and personal information. A good test is to ask a personal business related question. For example; if you are presenting at an in home sale, you may say after telling your story, "You know it has just occurred to me that you obviously know what it is that I do for a living but I don't know what it is that you or your spouse do." You should get the response you need, and this could be a very important piece of information to have. You wouldn't want to get into a dialogue if you were unfamiliar in an area of the prospects expertise. On the other hand you could allow the prospect to support your position by utilizing that information to your advantage. For example you may say, actually Mr. Prospect since you are an engineer you probably know exactly how this is done don't you? Note: always keep probative or supportive statements in the form of a question or you will lose control The fact that you asked instead of told, allows you to come back after the prospect has had his time to participate and give his answer with a simple rhetorical like "exactly that is why" and then go on once again in control. You also now have them engaged in the process.

In addition I use this time to explain or lay out what it is I will be trying to accomplish in this presentation, including the fact that I intend to get the sale. As you get each point across you button it up or close it. For example, you spent time explaining your company and what it has done and can do, you now ask, is this the kind of company you want to do business with? If you get a yes and you should, you have closed that part of the sale. If you received a no then needless to say, you should not go further until you uncover the objection and handle it to the point that you get a yes.

The last phase of this step will be to actually get permission to go on in your presentation with the understanding that you intend to close the deal.

An example of how I end this step is in the form of a statement, followed by a simple question.

Mr. and Mrs. Prospect it is my intention to spend as much time as you want to give you all the information that you will need in making a valued decision. Please don't hesitate to ask me any questions you may have. In addition to the information I will be giving I will also give you a to the penny price that will be good for say X number of days.

I also want you to know that if and when the time comes, I am in a position to offer and save you a considerable amount of savings today. All I ask in return is this, at some point I will ask you a question, and all I want is a Yes or a No answer to that question, and so you know, I can take a yes just a graciously as a no. I end this statement with this "Fair Enough". This can invoke a quick okay, or it may open a complete defense statement or it may uncover a strong objection, good bring it on, the quicker you can get the objections out of the way the better off you are. Almost always though it is answered with "yes that seems fair".

How to handle objections will be described later in the closing and in a summary.

Whenever the yes comes be it immediately, which actually will happen much more often then not, or after more dialogue it does not matter, as long as it comes. Do not go on until you get the OK. The permission to go on is critical to the conclusion of this step and the entire presentation.

For some of you this may seem a bit too strong, it is not! When properly done if you have warmed up with the prospect, it is as smooth as silk and no problem. One of the things I do if things do not feel as warm to me as they should be, I add to the end of question, the following statement Thank you for your response, now I'm sure we will be able to work together. This will soften the pre-close.

All I can say in conclusion of this step is that once you have received the OK to ask this Yes or No question you are going to be a successful closer. In truth you just closed the deal and all that is left to do is to give them what they want.

From this point on all you are going to do is show and build the value and satisfy the wants and needs.

Let's start with satisfying why they want to do business with your company.

7 - THE COMPANY STORE

This should be pretty straightforward but the way you relay the information is very important.

As a representative of your company you should be extremely enthusiastic and you should be able to give company history in a very interesting and entertaining manner. Some of the information the Prospect will need to know are, how the company was formed, when it was formed, why it was formed, how it is that it is positioned to do what it is in business to do. This would be the time to show referrals and share awards or affiliations like Better Business.

An example of a great company story is one I used to tell when I was selling roofing products. My company was valued in status by my including and telling a vendor story, it went like this. At the XYZ Company we can use all kinds of roofing materials but we choose to use the products from a company that was founded back in 1856, it was started by a group of twelve men who were painters. At some point they were painting roofs and in the process they learned how to add a rubber compound into the paint, which was a far better way to resurface a leaky roof. It was agreed that if they sprinkled some crushed stone onto the rubberized paint it was not only easier to walk on but it added longevity. After a while they learned that they could prepare this material into sheets ahead of time, and thus the rolled roofing industry was created. Later those same rolls were cut up into smaller more manageable pieces called shingles. This company has grown to be a leader in the industry. This story made it enjoyable and added creditability to my company and me.

Now not everyone works for a major and well-known name but every company has a history, which can be told in an informative and interesting way. It is ok to talk about any adversity the company may have faced as long as you can turn them into positives. It is far better then having the prospect bring it up at a critical time like in closing. This would put you on the defensive and in sales and you always want to be on the offense. You need to know all the basics like all the important phone numbers, the company address, the address for shipping, and warehousing if different, including the zip codes. You should also be able to relay the names and phone numbers of all key people and departments.

In conclusion you want to ask if the prospect wants to know anything else you may have not told them about the company.

After agreeing that you have provided the prospect with all the company information, ask 'is this the kind of company you would like to do business with'. When they say yes make some notes including that they like the company and move on to your product or service.

It is sometimes better to ask the prospect what it is that they look for when deciding with whom they want to do business. This allows them to sell themselves on doing business with you. This is especially effective if the prospect is not engaging.

8 - THE PRODUCT OR SERVICE/MEASURE

Since this is not a product specific book, this chapter will be written in general terms. Interestingly the product or service is not the key to your success. The key is the way you present the product or service, your knowledge, belief and commitment to it.

First and foremost you must truly believe in what you are selling. Knowing that everyone in sales should feel the same way, it stands to reason that the person who gets the prospect to agree that their products or services has value to them, should have the advantage and get the sale in the end. You need to do a masterful presentation. When selling a product or service you always have to present features. A feature however without a benefit to the prospect is worth nothing. You need to be conscious of the prospects reactions to a feature and benefit. Once you deliver the feature and benefit seek to get a physical or verbal approval. You should always look for and make sure you share with the prospect those features and benefits that are what I call un-shopable.

I was working in New York City at a high-end specialty store selling convertible sofa beds. There were many furniture stores near the shop, all within minutes of each other. All of them sold Sofa Beds, each had features and benefits to talk about. As I did my demonstration I would express that we had styles no one else had but most of all, I told them that when they shopped at a competitors they should look to see if they could find two things; the first was what I called a "recessed fold bar" I had the prospect lay down on the bed but before they did, I folded back the mattress to show how the center support bar was turned in a downward position. Now as they were on the bed I asked, "Do you feel the bar", of course I knew they would not. Then while they were on the mattress I would ask one of them to role on their side and I asked the other if they noticed that they had not felt the movement. They would answer that they could not. I would reply, that is because of the spring system we use, it is a "Permerlater Grid spring system". I had found out from the manufacture of the mattress that the helical springs were tied together with a wire that created a grid pattern that allowed the springs to work independently of each other. He called it a "Permerlater". I generally closed 70% of my attempts before they left the shop, but for the ones that wanted to look around, I made sure they had those two un-shopable features imbedded in their minds. I in fact told them to be sure to lie down so they could feel the bar in their back and be sure to ask if the competitor's product had a "Permerlater". The fact is most of the beds on the market were made close to the exact spring system. I keyed in on the term "Permerlater Grid" and because of my attention to the details in doing my Pre-Sale step, I had the advantage over the competition because they had no idea of what it was. Of those customers who went elsewhere 80% came back and purchased from me. 100% of them said the other sales people didn't do as thorough a presentation and they were clueless when they mentioned the "Permerlater Grid". Make sure you present exclusive and un-shopable features.

Once you are confident that you have the prospects confidence in your product or service, you need to make it affordable. The way you achieve affordability is to show them the value. How value is achieved will be detailed in the next chapter, Power of Pen and paper.

Not all but generally, products and or services have evolved from some other product or service. It is a good thing to show or point out this evolution. It shows that you have experience and helps to justify why they should do business with you. As an example of selling evolution I again will draw on my own experience. I will once again be talking about a spring system, this time in an upholstery line.

For years I was selling spring systems that were hand tied with a sisal twine. Which was thought to be the best way to build a seat. The problem is that eventually the sisal broke down and labor costs of hand trying brought the cost through the roof. Eventually the system was replaced with a drop in system and the coils are now link tied together with a metal staple like tie. During a trade show a buyer of a major department store expressed that they preferred our old hand tie system and asked, why we made the change. After cautiously pointing out a few negatives to the hand tie system, I stated that we had evolved our product to a much stronger but equally as comfortable system. Simply put, I said that it's like this, the horse and buggy was a good way to travel for years but you just can't get to the moon that way. Well that brought a smile to her face and a rather large order to follow.

I also like to point out that perception is a very important element with all aspects of the sales process, particularly so when presenting your product or service. If you believe there is a negative with your product it is up to you to turn that to a positive. At the very least you should point it out and at the same time show a positive that out weighs that negative. The key is to point it out before the prospect does. In example, while representing Carter Industries, a very progressive contemporary upholstery manufacturers, they had introduced a sofa that could be put together by the homeowner. When first introduced the fabric was only available in a khaki color sailcloth. It was a huge success. At the following furniture market the company added three additional colors to the line. Prior to the opening of the show the issue or negative for some of the sales force was brought up during our showroom walk through. The original khaki sofa went up in cost by $25.00 and the colors were $75.00 more than that. Since I had one of the highest volumes of shipments of this product, the sales manager turned to me and asked what I thought. He wanted to know how I would present the new colors and the price increase to my attending dealers. I simply said I would quote the price of all colors at the higher price and then I would enthusiastically announce that we had a special on the khaki saving them $75.00. Like I said it's not what it is, it is all how it is perceived and approaching the pricing in this way for me did wipe away any negative. One more comment about price. Keep in mind that it is the value, not the price that we are selling. Yesterday's price is old to you but it's new to the prospect. When presenting the product be creative but keep it factual.

CAUTION: Never make a statement or claim without the supporting materials to back up the claim.

I mention Measure (evaluation by another name) as part of this chapter. In the home improvement industry Measure is a physical element designed to create or enhance need. In a service-oriented sale it is the same. Want and Need are of course two separate elements, both are needed to achieve a successful result. For example if you are selling replacement windows you would want to know the size of an opening in order to insure a proper fit. So you measure but at the same time you should look to see if there is rotten wood, gaps that would allow for air infiltration, and if the sashes are painted shut or not operable in any way. By doing this you have the ammo needed to take a want and add a need. Similarly you will need to do the same in selling your service. If you are selling insurance you will need to examine current policies to see if they fulfill their requirements, and as you do, based upon the information you have learned in the prior steps, point out the short falls to create the need.

You will conclude with product, service and measure as you revisit your product's features and benefits so it satisfies their needs and their wants. Whether you do the measure or analysis before or after the product demonstration is entirely up to you it does not matter, as long as you tie it into what it is that you are selling. As a trial close in concluding this aspect you want to ask, "So if price were not an object and based on all that we have discussed, is this the type of product or service you would like to have". "Yes". "Well that is great?"

Remember this, prospects buy on want, need and most importantly emotion. In almost every instance product presentation is the only time you can achieve this involvement.

9 - THE POWER OF THE PENCIL AND PAD

From beginning to end you should have had your pen and paper working. I find that making notes as we progress accomplishes many things but more than anything it makes the prospect comfortable in watching me write things down.

As we set sale and stay on the course I will write all the important points and all the commitments we make to each other. Considering that in the end your goal is to be writing an agreement getting your prospect comfortable with you writing is a good idea.

The power of the Pencil and Pad also includes presenting warranties and other legal forms like insurances certifications, spec sheets, licensees and items of that nature. I also use Power of the Pencil and Pad to price condition, by showing comparable information or competitors pricing at this phase. Lastly this is when you want to show how doing business with you makes sense. You will in this step give them hard numbers designed to show the value or the Return on the Investment (ROI). For example if the product is going to add energy efficiency savings on maintenance and real-estate value to the home, I would calculate those savings then get the prospect to agree on the numbers. Those numbers will then be used in creating the cost versus the value, or the ROI. The key is to have all numbers on paper and to have the numbers completely understood and agreed upon. It is important that even if you know your numbers are one hundred percent correct, it is fine to use a lesser number as long as the prospect is comfortable and agrees with those numbers. In the end whatever number it is it will show payback. Now you can begin to wrap things up and you're ready to review what you have laid out.

10 - REVIEW AND BUTTON UP GET READY TO CLOSE

After every thing has been presented and you are confident you have made all the points guess what, here we go again. After making a transition statement, for example, so we have covered quite a bit and shared lots of information, would you agree? This should get a positive response like, 'yes we did'. Yes I agree, what I would like to do now is make sure I have not omitted something and that all the information is correct, this is the door opener to presenting a complete review. Review or Layering is another way to describe this next step in our journey. Layering and reviewing is accomplished by asking questions, and then stating supporting facts. Here is a basic example.

We did agree that based on what we discussed my company is the kind of company you would like to do business with correct. Great!

Then let me make sure that I'm correct on what your expectations will be from my company and me. We will be removing all of your old siding and hauling it away. Then we will be installing wall leveling fan fold insulation. Then we will apply the XYZ lifetime warranted double four wood-grained virgin vinyl siding. You get the gist. As you recap or layer, you are assuming the sale and you are getting a yes or positive response as you go. You are conditioning your prospect, in preparation to close, all of the recapping and getting the prospect to agree is essential. The most important outcome in this step is that you are subliminally price conditioning. Once you are sure that you covered everything you needed to, you are ready to close. At this point it is a good to have them relaxed. You may need to take a quick break if you don't have a beverage now would be a good time to ask for some water, if you have some finish it and ask for more. After the break I would actually say something like this, well then I guess I have everything I need to figure this proposal out. While I do the numbers, why don't you look at this book, you can see some of our work and read some testimonials. When I am done we can have some fun and do all that we can to make all of this so it's affordable for you, Fair Enough! Now you're ready to go to The Close.

11 - CLOSE THE FUN PART

Closing really should be the easiest part of this trip. If you Set Your Sale's and follow the course including a properly delivered Pre-Close, you actually already closed. Basically you started out from your mooring in the port and now you're returning to the same port and ready to tie it all up at the same mooring.

So here is what we have done so far on our journey.

• We did all the preparation before the call.

• We established want and need.

• We conditioned for price, created or establish the value.

Now we need to navigate our way through the harbor and make it happen and affordable. After all is said and done it should and will always come down to the price, (affordability and value) as they say, "Show Me the Money".

Once again I cannot express enough how much you need to be calm and relaxed, and remember this is not about you, its now and is always been about them, especially at this point. The best way to achieve this is not to shortcut, do a masterful presentation and cover all of the steps. You must have total belief in what you have demonstrated.

Understanding this is not about you, it is always about what is best for the prospect, will keep you focused on getting the sale without applying pressure. Now before delivering the price use what you established with the power of the Pencil and Pad.

On the same page that you did ROI or your price justification, write down the full price, do it so the prospect can see what you are doing but disguise the number so it is yours to know and theirs to find out. What this means is since it is all about the Money you should hold back on any discounts or specials you may be able to offer. Now let the prospect know that you have written the total down and then ask the prospect to take a guess. Say something like are you ready for the fun part, Ok then based on all that we discussed and agreed on, and after seeing comparable pricing what do you think the fair price will be? You will be amazed at the various responses.

If they guess higher, great you know you price conditioned well. If the guess is too low that's fine, all you have to say is something like "you are an optimist" the actual price is just a bit more. In most cases the low guess is just to let you know they know it's more but they are ready to negotiate. However, you should be conscious of the fact that they just may not have grasped the price conditioning you discussed. So when the guess is lower, just to be on the safe side, go back to show value, repeat your layering items, discuss national, regional pricing or whatever comparison you showed previously, then once again point out the un-shopable features that you had to offer.

When you are finally ready to offer up the price, you do it by showing the number you have written down, now be positive and assumptive and without hesitation, offer that the way you can precede is by taking a payment, a small deposit now, and explain that the balance can be paid by whatever terms you can and want to present them. If you are offering financing (highly recommended) you should first offer the price in terms of equal cash payments at this time in terms of, 50/50 or 1/3 down and so on. The best way to offer financing is to make a statement of common fact. I would say after giving the cash price, again without hesitation, "Or you can do what almost all my clients do". They use my great financing and continue to offer those options and offer up payments.

In example say the total price of the project is $9,000. You would show the cash price of $9,000 with a third down of $3,000 and the balance paid upon completion or delivery. Or I can take $100.00 down and depending which plan you prefer I can offer you easy payments of $225.00, $180.00 or $75.00 per month which would you prefer? It is essential that once you have explained the payment options that you say nothing. Sit back and relax, say nothing, wait for them to speak, if you don't you might as well jump overboard. The person who speaks first will almost always be the loser.

At this point you're going to get them to say ok

lets do it. If so great! You had done a masterful job and were rewarded with the beloved "Lay Down" no other closing is necessary. Shake hands and Write it up.

More often then not you will get some objection and need to go to work now. There are lots of objections, I will share several of them and offer ways to handle them in the next chapter. The key is not to go to next close attempt until you have isolated the objections and over come those objections. You need to isolate and satisfy all their objections bringing it to the one and most important objection, most often the price or commonly known as the money. In the paragraphs below I will offer a scenario based on two objections that come up most often. I will isolate, then overcome them so I can go to close. Remember this, the key to overcoming objection is Isolation.

PROSPECT: Objection, well that all sounds good but we need to <u>think about it</u> and I have to <u>wait for two months</u> so I can use my bonus to help with down payment.

SALES PRO: I understand, no problem. So I understand exactly, you are good with everything else however you need time to get your <u>money</u> together and in two months you will have the money is that correct.

PROSPECT: Yes

SALES PRO: So if I had a way so you could get the work done and you wouldn't have to pay for it now. Let's say if I could arrange that <u>you didn't need to pay</u> for it for six months, you could and would <u>want to do it</u>.

PROSPECT: Yes

SALES PRO: Well congratulations I can get that done for you, for a limited time I can offer 12 months same as cash program, I will need to call my Operations Manager for the approval I will call now!

PROSPECT: Well that sounds good but I am still not sure I want to <u>spend</u> that much.

SALES PRO: I understand no problem. Let me ask you this. It seems to me that you really like my products or service is that correct.

PROSPECT: Yes

SALES PRO: And if not now at some point you are going to move forward with this project.

PROSPECT: Yes

SALES PRO: And you did say that my company is the kind of company you want to do business with, correct?

PROSPECT: Yes

SALES PRO: Then I guess the last and only thing that's keeping us from moving forward is the <u>Money</u> isn't it?

PROSPECT: Yes

That's it, you just isolated all the objections and now you will close.

SURPRISE!

Go back to Chapter Six, **THE PRE-CLOSE**

Well great! Remember way back when we first got started? I told you that I was here to give you as much information as I could and I would try to answer all of your questions and I would do that, so that you could make a valued decision? Yes. Well have I answered all of your questions? Yes. Great! Do you also remember what I said; if and when that time came I was in a position to save you some money if we did business today? Yes. The only thing I asked in return was that you give me a yes or no to a simple question and you said you would do that, correct/ yes, well this is the time. One last thing, you did say that the $180.00 payment was going to be comfortable and affordable for you correct? Yes... Ok then, the price I just quoted you is going to be good for 30 days. The question I need the yes or no to is simply this. If I can get the cost down so you would be happy and it is more than affordable, and you did not have to pay for it until after you received you bonus, can we get started within the next two weeks. Yes or No? Get the yes then do the math. Let's say you could do 20% off. You deliver the price like this. Say Wow! Congratulations. The regular price is $9,000.00. The price I can do for today only is $7,200.00 wow, that's a huge saving of $1,800 and the payment on that is now actually less than $180.00 it is only $150.00 per month that's less than even I expected. Now keep quiet again let them answer first no matter how long it takes.

PROSPECT: That sounds good.

SALES PRO: Great! Shake the hand and write the paper!

Now you know the power of the Pre-Close. Notice that the question was directed by time assuming that the price had to be ok as long as I could do it in the next two weeks. This allows the prospect a little wiggle room so they remain comfortable. Assume they answered well that depends on the price. The Pre-Close allows you to be in a position of control without pressure. Your response I understand, but I can assure you that you will like the price. I just need to know if the two-week start will be ok with you. By not debating price, the Pre-Close is the secret of getting them to comfortably commit to you. Master this and you will be in command of your ship.

Knowing that you have done everything you need to going from Pre-Sale to Close will enable you to handle almost all objections. Give an absolute and Masterful Presentation do this with the understanding that it is all about them and you will archive selling success.

12 - COMMON OBJECTIONS

Over the years I have heard some pretty good objections. More then I can even begin to remember. Over the next few paragraphs I will share some of them with you.

It is important to keep in mind that you will need to be patient; understanding and you must spend whatever time is needed to isolate each objection before you attempt the close. When overcoming an objection there are some cautions to consider. You should never use words that can create hostility or pressure, do not argue your point. Keep the response so it is open ended. The best way I found to accomplish overcoming impatience a concern about closing is to once again keep in mind, this is not about you, and it is all about satisfying the prospect.

Will you be able to overcome an objection every time? No absolutely not. Do it better then 70% of the time and you will be a Sales leader. One more thing on getting a No, a No today is not necessarily a No tomorrow! Don't give up, keep in touch with the prospect for they represent possible future business.

When you, shortcut the system, you run the risk of not being able to overcome objections. How so; 1 - If you do not take the time to warm up you will not have the prospects trust. 2 - If you do not take the time to build the value you are not giving the prospect a reason to do business with you and or your company. 3 - If you have not engaged the prospect in the process you cannot get them emotionally involved with the product or service. If you leave any or all of these steps out, it will make handling an objection very difficult and can become combative. So if you find that you are having difficulty overcoming objections, I suggest you do a little soul searching and if you are shortcutting, you may actually be the objection.

If you followed the steps with the best interest of the prospect in mind, you will be able to overcome most objections.

Listed below are many of the objections I have had to overcome, I'm sure you can think of more.

MOST COMMON OBJECTIONS:

1. I want to think it over
2. I want to consult a third party
3. I have other priorities
4. I can't afford it
5. I don't like financing
6. I want to get my own financing
7. I never make a decision in one day
8. I can't decide on the color, size, shape, etc.
9. I need to get other prices
10. That's more than I wanted to spend

HANDLING THE OBJECTION

A common come back to all of the above is, "I understand, no problem". Then you want to ask an open ended question or a series of questions. An example to objection number 10 that is more than I wanted to spend. Your response is I understand no problem! Let me ask you this though, if price were no object would I be the person you would like to make your purchase from? Yes. Then I assume you would feel the same way about my company? Yes. Once again if you don't mind, if price was not the issue, this is the product or service you would want. Yes so then it really is just the money that is keeping us apart. Yes. (Now get a price from them that they will agree to.) Well congratulations I am in a position to meet that price. Note the price concession must be conditional and closed in time.

What happened in this entire dialogue was it isolated the prospects objection in a non-pressured non-combative way.

The way you open is the way you close. Remember the rule is isolate. Other non-combative ways to overcome the objection is to offer help; you do this with some common closes.

COMMON CLOSES

FEEL FELT FOUND CLOSE:

The Feel Felt Found close is designed to help bring in a third party or an experience you can share that will take away the concern or objection. It is very simple. All you say in response is, "I know exactly how you feel, I felt the exact same way, however this is what I found. Then you simply satisfy the objection with positive feed back.

BEN FRANKLIN CLOSE:

The Bed Franklin close is the best way to handle a think it over objection. Ben was of course a very inventive and analytical person. To open on this close, you again say, I understand, no problem. In order to help you I have a formula that has helped so many other people who want to think things over before giving the ok. Let me share this with you. Now you make two columns on one side you put the negatives and on the other you put all the positives. By doing this one simple task you bring out all the possible things to think about. Your objective is to do this in such a way that it works toward isolating the real item they wanted to think about, that of course is the Money. It's always the money!

PIE CLOSE:

Use this for the Too Much Money objection it will show value. Draw a circle that's the pie. Now cut the pie in pieces based on all those things you layered, all those items they will be getting by doing business with you. You justify your price and show the value by removing pieces of the pie. This gives real value to those items. Another name for this close is the Take Away Close.

FINANCING CLOSE: (My Favorite)

The finance close is the best way to make a purchase affordable. The, I can't afford it objection is blown away. The best way to close is with financing and the best way to do this is to give or show three different ways in which a product or service can be purchased. Generally you will use this close, believe it or not to overcome the, I don't like to finance objection. The first thing you do is to write down and show what it would take to purchase in cash. Explain those terms and show the dollar amount on the same paper assume a comfortable down payment and show two different monthly payments based on rates and terms. Then you simply ask which method they would be comfortable with. If they objected to those payments or terms you say, "No problem, I understand." But let me ask you on cash flow basis what would you be comfortable with? Get the answer, rework your number and make it happen.

Another way to use Financing as a close is to offer assurance of a satisfied job. With the use of financing all the prospect need to do is to give a small deposit, then based on the credit approval all the work is performed. At the completion of the work the prospect will be asked to OK a completion form before the funds are released to the company. Thus it gives the assurance of a job done well.

There are videos, auto tapes and publications on closings and I know most if not all of them. Who knows, I may some day do tapes on closing myself. For now keep in mind the key to handling objections and closing sales is to set back relax and enjoy the ride. The point was made earlier all you need to do is follow the steps in this system, it is the only way it will work. Follow the steps and Isolate all objections and you will close sales. Don't be a robot though, use your personality, your words and think outside the box, be creative and above all, have fun. Do this and enjoy the rewards as you Set Your Sales in an exciting ever changing career in sales.

13 - DEALING WITH DIFFERENT PEOPLE

It takes two to tango, oil and vinegar don't mix, night and day, opposites attract. That's what makes the world go around. So we are confronted with many different types of people. In a perfect world we would all be able to get along but the truth is we don't.

So I try to be a chameleon. As I laid out earlier in the Pre-Sale preparation, it is extremely helpful as an aid to getting along with a wide and varied group of personalities. Reading and staying on top of current events and on what's going on in your market place will give you the ability to be a bit of a chameleon.

Over my years and from lots of hands on experiences and by attending many training seminars, I have been able to identify and categorize some different personalities I will share them in an attempt to give you just a bit of insight. I am not trying to name call here just a guide to help you navigate the course.

THE KNOW IT ALL:

Yep you guessed it, the person who has all the answers, they know more than you do. This person may even be a person that at one time or another was in some way affiliated in you particular business.

The reason for this person's behavior is that they do not like to be out done. They also know that with a good closer like you they are toast.

The best thing to do with this person is to let them sell themselves. Let them tell you all about your products all you should do is enthusiastically agree with them. And get ready to close.

THE YES MAN- WOMEN:

The nice thing about this person they say yes to every thing you say or do. The bad news is they usually have made a decision that no matter what you do or say to them they are not going to make a purchase from you. I found that the reality is that this person is scared to let their guard down knowing that if they do, you will close them. The best way to get them out of the yes mode is to kill the fear and bring them to reality and help them to face the fear. What I do is to flat out ask them why they won't be buying from me today. This question sends lightning bolts through them and puts you back in control of the process.

THE HIGH ROLLER:

This person wants to impress and control you by telling you how much they own and who they know.

The High Roller will tell you how important they are and in most cases be draped in gold and diamonds. For the most part I have found that this person is living high above their means. They are basically asking, no better yet, they are crying for help. Be wise play along don't ask for money, instead ask how long it will take to free up some assets. The best thing to do with this type of person is go along for the ride, in the end you better have all your financing tools with you including any debt consolidation tools. Do this like they are your best friend and you will close almost every time.

These are just a few of the many types of buyers that are out there. Yes I said buyers, if you spend the time, do your homework and preparation, and if you follow the system, the personalities should not matter.

14 - SUMMARY AND WRAP UP

In wrapping up I want to point out that like anything in life practice makes perfect. My expectations for this book were to set a short uncomplicated outline to follow and digest, I hope I have done so. I know it's short but if you think all you need to do is read it once and you instantly become a strong closer it won't happen. You need to practice and be repetitive and in understating each step make it your own. I am a believer that repetition is the motor of learning. So review the steps over and over practice until you own them. It seems that in most companies the larger percentage of sales people are closing at 40% or less. If you own this process I'm sure you will close far more than 50%, 60 % or even 70% of the time. I suggest that you tape yourself and review your presentation on a monthly basis or more if needed. Your success and income will be in your destiny and you will achieve true independence.

Not meaning to confuse anyone, yes this is a system a methodology but it is important to understand we are not and we are not dealing with robots. Inject your personality in all that you do. Be creative and think out of the box. If you do you will be able to overcome most of what life throws at you.

So allow me to share one last story and share an example of how I was thinking out side the box and how it helped me to overcome a hard time. It all started in the 1980's. I had been promoted from an associate sales representative and was presented with a territory as a factory direct representative. This as in most good sales opportunities was a commission only position. The territory I was given meant an eventual move. Before uprooting my wife and two year old daughter, I went on the road off to conquer the world. This territory was presented to me as a great opportunity, in other words it was not at all established. At the time of my take over the best yearly yield was $150,000. I worked hard in making the rounds trying to build rapport and peek interest in my line. I had started in months ahead working to drive dealers to see me at the furniture market taking place in High Point NC. Finally it was time to receive the fruits of my labor, the show was just a few days from opening. I was fired up and ready to go, I anticipated a large turn out at the show.

Not so fast. It was one of the biggest disappointments of my young life. I was anticipating a great show when the then president Ronald Regan addressed the nation and announced the worst recession in recent history. Well it was a disaster the show was a bust and the confidence in the economy was lost. Not only did I not get new business I was losing dealers. No one wanted to buy my furniture. That was it no one wanted to buy furniture. I was eating dinner at a hotel I frequently stayed at while working in Syracuse NY. Suddenly and without warning it hit me. No one wanted to buy furniture but as I sat and looked through the dining room I had seen a board. On that board were 100 boxes yep you guessed it, it was a Supper Bowl pool. With only two weeks to go I contacted the President of my company and told him that no one wanted to buy furniture but maybe they would give me a shot and enter my pool, for every one thousand dollars in orders they gave me they could pick a box. If they won they get ten thousand dollars in cash or in company credit. It meant a 10% discount to the factory. It was approved and in two weeks and what was one of the worst economic times ever, I had sold over $100,000. It was a huge success for my company and me. This move led to a huge increase in the territory. Always look for the possibilities, and have fun with a life in sales, it's all up to you.

Some final rules to remember, attitude is everything, be energetic but not loud and offensive. Be confident through knowledge don't be arrogant and cocky. It is ok to believe in yourself and there is nothing wrong with inner arrogance in so much as you will do what it takes to be successful. Never argue a point, persuade don't force. Be thankful and gracious.

15 - PROSPECTING

Prospecting is the lifeline to your success in sales. It is always nice to be handed a lead, however if you are solely dependant on leads it will hinder your earning and limit your success.

Prospecting for sales will take some effort, but it will pay huge dividends. There are many ways to prospect. Getting referrals is the best way and it is the easiest to attain, you simply ask for them from customers you have satisfied. Getting a past customers endorsement is huge in getting instant trust. Be creative go to trade shows, advertise on the social media sites. Just talk to people, let them know what it is you do. Hand out business cards and flyers. All it takes is effort. Far too many talented sales people fall by the way side and many lesser talented people achieve great success form this one element alone. So prospect and excel.

SUMMARY AID

OPENING:
- Get Control
- State the value of your visit
- Bonding

QUALIFYING:
- Ask questions
- Find the want
- Create the need
- Uncover facts and circumstance

SATISFYING:
- It's all about them
- Show the benefits
- Gain trust and acceptance

CLOSE:
- Pre-Close, set it up early
- Review the facts gain the value
- Layering, show the pro's
- Ask for the order

OVERCOMING OBJECTION:
- Confirm the objection and Isolate
- Explore the solutions
- Repeat and conclude

Some tips on words to use and avoid in sales, especially when closing or handling an objection are listed below.

WORDS PAINT THE PICTURE

Don't Use	Do Use
Contract	Paperwork, Agreement
Sign	Ok, Approve
Deal	Opportunity
Cost	Investment
Down Payment	Initial Investment
Problem	Challenge
Commission	Fee for Service

<u>NOTES</u>

ABOUT THE AUTHOR

I am now retired and volunteering with a wonderful help group assisting others in startups. I have enjoyed the best of times and some hard times too. One thing I have always enjoyed throughout my life is that I have always been in control of my own destiny. My career in sales has given me an inner confidence and feeling of security that I just don't think I could have achieved if I chose to do something else in life. I am grateful for all that. In Retirement I also intend to train and mentor on a fee for service basis. If you would like some first hand training drop me an email at bobrusso21@gmail.com